I&DOG

Photography by John Sann and Monique Stauder

YORKVILLE PRESS
NEW YORK, NEW YORK

Library of Congress Cataloging-in-Publication Data

I & dog / Monks of New Skete.
p. cm.
ISBN 0-9729427-3-4
1. Dogs. 2. Dogs--Pictorial works. 3. Human-animal relationships.
I. Title: I and dog. II. Monks of New Skete. III. Title.
SF426.2.I5 2003
636.7--dc22
2003017520

jes 10 9 8 7 6 5 4 3 2 1

DESIGN BY: Tina Taylor

PHOTOGRAPHS © BY: John Sann
Pages; 6-7, 8, 11, 14, 16-17, 20-21, 26, 27, 28-29, 32-33, 34, 38-39, 42, 46-47, 48, 52, 54, 56, 57, 64, 67, 72, 74, 75, 77, 80

PHOTOGRAPHS © BY: Monique Stauder
Cover; Pages; 1, 3, 4, 12, 18, 22, 23, 24, 31, 37, 40-41, 44, 50, 51, 58, 61, 62-63, 68, 71, 78, 79

PRINTED BY: Friesens in Canada

I&DOG

the monks of new skete

INTRODUCTION

In 1923 Jewish philosopher Martin Buber penned a work that has become a perennial classic in the philosophy of religion: *I and Thou*. Taking issue with a narrow understanding of spirituality and mysticism, Buber presented God radically as the Eternal Thou, whom we can truly meet in all our relationships, and not only in solitude.

Readers familiar with Buber may smile at our allusion to him in *I & Dog,* but in fact the inspiration is real. Buber's central intuition is that how we are in relationship with everything in our lives affects our experience of the sacred, and that we realize this effect in the very act of relationship, if only we are open. We humans can and do form mutually inspiring and beneficial relationships with our dog companions, and this experience colors every aspect of our life.

Yet the burden is not entirely on us to create or invent this marvelous reality. The tradition in which we stand believes that we already exist in a profound communion with all that is. Somehow, most of the time, we seem to stop growing in our awareness of this vital reality, of being truly at home in our bodies, and with each other, and in the cosmos. Constantly we become distracted and rarely do we listen.

Our dog friends, like life itself, are trying to get our attention. Maybe our canine connection is the missing link, a crucial invitation to respond to this great call to a richer, more abundant banquet of life that is already prepared and waiting.

For many of us, love for creation deepens through

the relationships we form with our pets, particularly our dogs.

BY THEIR VERY NATURE AND NEED, DOGS DRAW US OUT OF OURSELVES:

they root us in nature, making us more

conscious of the mystery of God

inherent in all things.

often our feelings about dogs arise out of deeply embedded memories from childhood when dogs assumed a multiplicity of roles: playmate, guardian, comic, even feared warrior down the street. The depth of such sensibilities, both positive and negative, point to the value of providing young children safe experiences with dogs at their best, when connections can be forged naturally, at their own pace.

PRAISE, THEN, IS MORE THAN TREATS,
MORE THAN AN OCCASIONAL PHYSICAL PAT,
AND MORE THAN A REWARD FOR GOOD ACTIONS.
PRAISE IS AN ATTITUDE, A STANCE. Dogs who live in an

atmosphere of praise come to love the human voice. They are more

trusting and accepting. They are approachable by strangers but not

demanding. Dogs confident of praise from their owners do not live

on the edge of an emotional abyss, always seeking attention,

and sulking when they do not get it. If praise is part of your attitude

toward your dog, you have a rich and exciting relationship ahead.

DOGS MIRROR US BACK TO OURSELVES IN
UNMISTAKABLE WAYS THAT, IF WE ARE OPEN,
FOSTER TRUE UNDERSTANDING AND CHANGE.
Dogs are guileless and filled with spontaneity: unlike people, they
don't deceive. When we take seriously the words they speak to us about
ourselves, we stand face to face with the truth of the matter. We must
learn to reflect on these words — they are inscribed on their bodies,
in their expressions, in the way they approach and interact with us.

In the book *Kinship With All Life*, J. Allen Boone went to visit

Mojave Dan, a wise old desert hermit who lived with a colony

of dogs and burros. He asked the hermit to help him understand his dog

and get at the truth of the animal. The sage thought for a while and then

answered, "THERE'S facts about DOGS, AND THERE'S OPINIONS ABOUT THEM. THE DOGS HAVE THE facts, AND THE HUMANS HAVE THE OPINIONS.

If you want facts about a dog, get them straight from the dog.

If you want opinions, get them from humans."

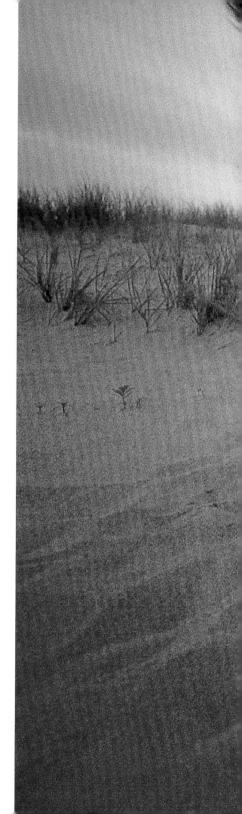

Often we blame our dogs for being disobedient

when the real problem lies with us.

BEING a GOOD tRaINER
anD a GOOD companion
ReQUIRES HUmILIty,

the humility to realize that our own handling

abilities with our dogs are continually developing;

it's always preferable to presume

that the problem lies with us.

Our world is increasingly afraid of silence, fearing the truths

it whispers in our consciences. But how silence can heal if we let it!

aLL good reLationships — those with our dogs
incLuded — wiLL make room for siLence,

for shared moments that transcend the need for speech. Silence allows us

to take account of ourselves, to change what is amiss, to renew our intention

to treat the other with the respect and affection characteristic of friendship.

People sometimes cringe at the thought of training, as if its purpose were to quench a dog's spirit. Nonsense. GENUINE TRAINING IS ABOUT FREEDOM: freedom for both ourselves and our dogs to enjoy each other, enhancing our relationships by allowing their potential to blossom in the patient context of trial and error, praise and appreciation.

Though it is entirely natural for us to project human motives onto dogs, ultimately this is unfair: it puts expectations on dogs that disregard their reality. DOGS WANDER IN THEIR OWN UNIVERSE AND RESIST BEING JUDGED ACCORDING TO HUMAN STANDARDS. We do justice to a relationship with a dog when we honor it as it is — a dog, a creature who, for all we may understand about it, is still fraught with mystery.

NOVELTY ISN'T ALWAYS DESIRABLE IN RELATING WITH A DOG. Dogs are sensitive to the security and comfort engendered by daily rituals we hardly give a second thought to: the morning walk, meal times, play sessions, even the quiet togetherness of evening TV.... Such familiar patterns stabilize the dog in a world it understands. THEY ALSO SOOTHE THE CHAOS OF OUR OWN LIVES BY THE PEACE THAT IS THEIR FRUIT.

Fathoming the way a dog develops means recognizing that

our knowledge reflects general patterns and not absolute rules.

we can never fully understand why
a dog is the way it is. In fact, "the dog" does not exist,

only individual dogs and the unique way each develops.

One thing about praise is to keep it sincere. DOGS CAN SPOT PHONINESS a mile away. For creatures that instinctively observe and interpret the slightest movements of body and soul, praise that is pure show leaves even a Labrador unmoved.

We do not find God solely in the interior realm, and when we live our lives as if we did, we fall victim to a dualism that has profound spiritual consequences. Because we are responsible for living creatures, needy and vulnerable, our dogs help ground us in reality, forcing us to appreciate the mystery of God in all its length and breadth.

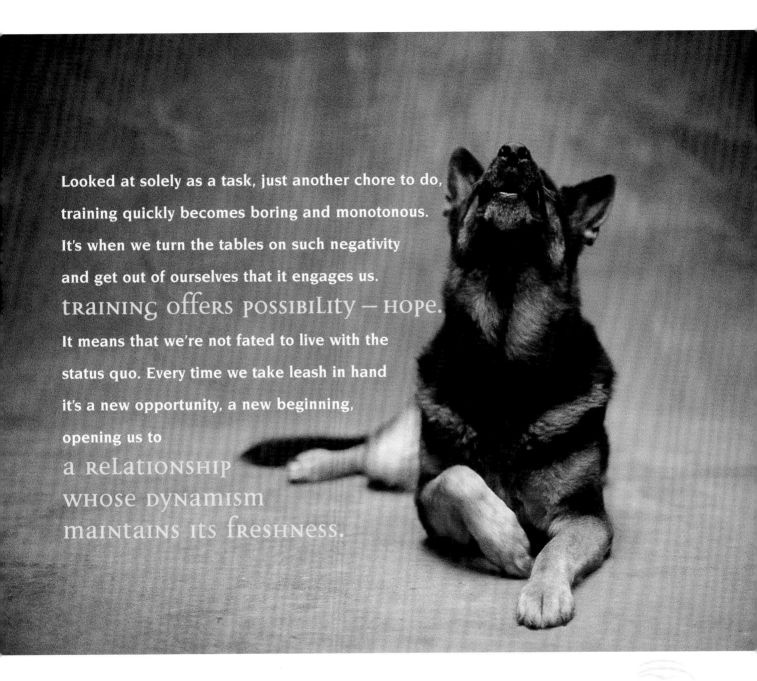

Looked at solely as a task, just another chore to do,
training quickly becomes boring and monotonous.
It's when we turn the tables on such negativity
and get out of ourselves that it engages us.
TRAINING OFFERS POSSIBILITY — HOPE.
It means that we're not fated to live with the
status quo. Every time we take leash in hand
it's a new opportunity, a new beginning,
opening us to
a RELATIONSHIP
WHOSE DYNAMISM
maintains its freshness.

33

From a spiritual perspective there is no limit to the change,

growth and maturity that a human being can undergo;

the wonder is that, in its own way, the same is true of the dog.

DOGS CAN ALWAYS GROW IN LEARNING AND RESPONSIVENESS, IN ATTENTIVENESS AND BONDING,

significantly broadening the parameters of what most of us

think is possible from a relationship.

Consider how a dog's eyes speak. They reflect a broad range of inner emotions that affect the quality of our relationship, if we care enough to listen. Joy, fear, curiosity, boredom and mischief are each reflected through the subtlest shifts in the dog's eyes.... Just as the New Testament teaches that "the eye is the lamp of the soul" in human beings, so to a certain extent can the same be said of the dog.

DOGS AND STICKS: IS THERE ANOTHER OBJECT TYPICALLY SO CLOSE AT HAND AS TO BECOME AN EFFORTLESS SOURCE OF DELIGHT FOR YOUR DOG?

A simple toss of a stick turns an ordinary walk into a game whose strategy is
to keep both of you fully engaged — your dog placing
the stick in the path of your leisurely walk, for example,
to solicit another toss; or daring you to pick it up before
its lightning-fast jaws sweep it away from your grasp.

Any healthy relationship involves the unexpected, the surprise that a break in routine can engender. Whether it's a spontaneous hike in the woods, a soothing massage, or even something special occasionally added to dinner, DOGS RELISH CREATIVE MOMENTS YOU DEVISE THAT SAY YOUR RELATIONSHIP IS NOT ON automatic.

Determination is a German shepherd refusing to

surrender a ball. Feeling the power contained in its jaws,

the vice-like strength and singleness of purpose,

HOW CAN ONE feeL ANYTHING BUT awe
WHEN MINUTES LATER THE BALL
IS LAID meekLy at YOUR feet?

what is it with the fetish
for dressing up dogs?

When people decorate them in outfits

of human silliness, do they ever consider

the canine ability to see through such mockery,

or do they even suspect their dogs' feelings of discomfort

and humiliation? DOGS DO NOt REQUIRE

SUCH VAIN attempts at makeover.

Their very nature possesses its own dignity,

transcending any need of supplement or change.

All that is required is our respect and admiration.

In a world choked with the disease of taking itself too seriously, dogs remind us of a more fundamental wisdom, which often eludes us in our self-preoccupation. ᴍᴏʀᴇ ᴛʜᴀɴ ᴀɴʏᴛʜɪɴɢ ᴇʟꜱᴇ, ᴅᴏɢꜱ ᴀʀᴇ ᴄʀᴇᴀᴛᴜʀᴇꜱ ᴏꜰ ᴘʟᴀʏ, ᴡʜᴏꜱᴇ ꜱᴘᴏɴᴛᴀɴᴇᴏᴜꜱ ɪɴᴛᴇʀᴀᴄᴛɪᴏɴ ᴡɪᴛʜ ʟɪꜰᴇ ʙᴇꜱᴘᴇᴀᴋꜱ ɪᴛꜱ ɢᴏᴏᴅɴᴇꜱꜱ. Dogs become what they are through play, through hours upon hours of undistracted merriment. No matter how serious their adult behavior becomes in hunting, guarding, roaming or working, the foundation always is play, and to play they return as to their proper home.

THE ROOT MEANING OF THE WORD OBEDIENCE IS "TO LISTEN." When applied to training our dogs, it involves as much our listening to the dog in order to discern what is needed, as it does the dog's responding to our commands. It involves laying aside our burdens for the moment and entering fully into the relationship here and now so that our word to the dog will be simple, clear, and free of emotional or physical static.

DOGS HAVE THEIR OWN RHYTHMS THAT ERUPT
SPONTANEOUSLY, EVEN WONDROUSLY:

a pair of amigos, for example, cavorting in the sand, relishing a rite of

mock combat, transforming primal energies into a joyous dance of celebration.

Dogs are often creatures of contradiction, boldly scaring off cars,

only to spook at the sight of a gently waving flag.

Their responses to life span a vast range of emotions,

which we know intimately in ourselves through the empathy they evoke.

Ultimately, dogs enchant us with their
honesty, a trait increasingly rare
in the nexus of relationships
that make up our lives.

part of the joy of getting a dog is naming it.

In Eden, Adam was given the responsibility of naming the animals,

and we have inherited this task. A name not only defines,

it expresses the hopes we bring to the relationship. Take care with a name;

Let its sound echo with delight in your soul,

for a name becomes the basis of countless acts of communication

that manifest your true feelings, regardless of whatever else is said.

DOGS ARE SUBJECTS IN THE KINGDOM OF NOW,
fULLy PRESENT TO THE PULSE of EACH moment.

Their behavioral rhythms shift as quickly as weather on a windy day.

Intense episodes of play and dominance that express a flurry of

activity one moment organically flow into a surrender to rest the next.

The dog knows only the present and offers itself to it without reserve.

When we are quiet enough, freed from all our inner noise and chatter, we can see with new respect the natural beauty and wisdom of the world around us and appreciate our ties to it. Such perceptive silence opens up our lives to a healthy reverence and awe for all things; it creates a capacity for openness that is both humanizing and life-giving.

Listen carefully to your life and you'll find that

companionship with a dog touches the broader issue of our relationship with all of creation and with the creator.

How we interact with a dog reflects our general attitude toward God and nature, a tell-tale sign of the soul.

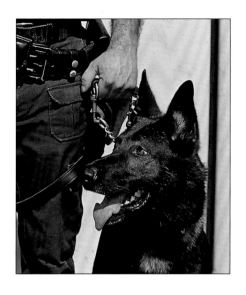

Those fortunate enough to be able to include their dog in their work know the impact this has on the relationship. Subtly, without even noticing, a familiarity and ease develops, making it difficult to imagine one's life without the presence of the other — not so much a shadow as a harmonious part of the landscape.

Over the years we've always been struck by the number of people who, all things considered, would rather spend time with a dog than with other human beings. Though pitting dogs against humans seems unwise, it is fair to ask: is there any other relationship in life in which the high point of the other's day is the moment we come home and walk through the door?

What other creature is so able to pierce the veneer of our defenses,

reducing the gruffest human being to unselfconscious displays

of laughter and fun? By their sheer spontaneity,

DOGS find our soft spots, keeping us
in touch with a more honest vision of
ourselves that doesn't buy its own facade.

The biggest problem with dogs is that they don't live long enough.

They always seem to leave us when we're most vulnerable,

most in need of their biased, affirming presence. DOGS make us

believe we can actually be as they see us,

and it's often only when they're gone that we realize

their role in what we've become.

BEING AUTHENTICALLY HUMAN
MEANS LEARNING TO GIVE OURSELVES
unselfishly and ungrudgingly. Isn't it surprising how
the nature of the dog evokes this from us in unique
and compelling ways? In the ordinary routine of a
relationship with a dog, through the discipline and
responsibility it entails, WE LEARN ABOUT
OURSELVES, ABOUT NATURE, ABOUT GOD
and the spiritual path we are on, in ways that would
otherwise be unavailable to us.

THE VULNERABILITY PRESENT IN THE SMALLEST OF GOD'S CREATURES CALLS OUT TO OUR NOBLEST INSTINCTS, triggering a desire to nurture and protect, to care for and understand. What we rarely imagine is how quickly the roles can change. Dogs have an astonishing capacity to respond to our own vulnerability, our sudden need for assistance. It's the flip side of a relationship written in paradox.

INSEEING IS STANDING IN YOUR DOG'S PSYCHE,
PUTTING YOURSELF AT HER CENTER, WHERE
SHE IS A UNIQUE, INDIVIDUAL CREATURE,
and understanding her from that perspective.... Inseeing is not a
romantic projection of human thoughts and feelings; it takes into account
the whole dog by reading what the major centers of communication
are saying: ears, eyes, mouth, tail, and body carriage.

Do the bonds of relationship extend beyond this life?

We have no proof, one way or another. But there is a depth

to our experience that awakens faith, faith that in the mysterious

character of life ultimately nothing of real value will ever be lost.

OUR CLOSEST RELATIONSHIPS,
BOTH WITH HUMANS AND WITH DOGS,
SOMEHOW POINT BEYOND THEMSELVES,
LEADING US TO HOPE THAT THERE IS INDEED
SOMETHING OF THE ETERNAL PRESENT IN THEM.

about the monks of new skete

The Monks of New Skete have lived as a religious community in Cambridge, New York, since 1967. They support themselves by breeding and training dogs at their monastery, and by making and selling specialty foods. They are the authors of *In the Spirit of Happiness: Spiritual Wisdom for Living,* and their best-selling guides to dog training, *How To Be Your Dog's Best Friend* and *The Art of Raising a Puppy*; and they've produced an award-winning video training series, *Raising Your Dogs With the Monks of New Skete.* For additional information, visit their website at www.newskete.com.

acknowledgments

We would like to thank all who participated in the making of this book: the dogs and their owners who played and posed for us, with a special thanks to the New York City Police Department and Officer Handley and K-9 Kiefer, who served as a search and rescue dog at the World Trade Center after the September 11, 2001, attack; the photographers John Sann and Monique Stauder; our publisher Kate Hartson, book designer Tina Taylor and editor Bob Somerville — and all our readers and clients over the years who continue to inspire us.

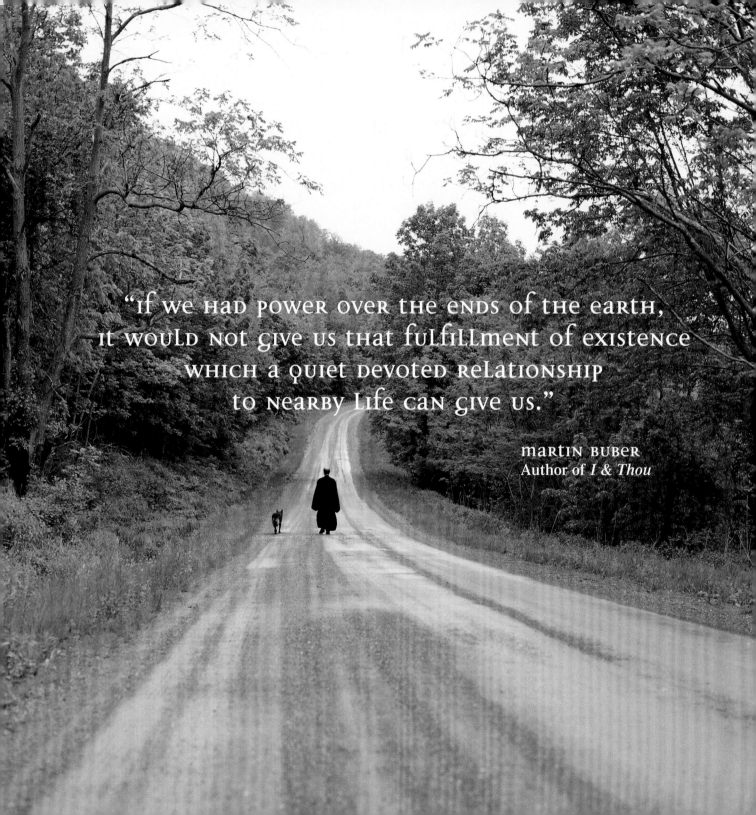

"If we had power over the ends of the earth, it would not give us that fulfillment of existence which a quiet devoted relationship to nearby Life can give us."

MARTIN BUBER
Author of *I & Thou*